THE STORY OF BRITAIN: FROM WILLIAM OF ORANGE TO WORLD WAR II

The author's lively approach to history and the artist's brilliant illustrations in both colour and black and white brings the past vividly to life in *The Story of Britain*, which was originally published as one volume.

The author, R. J. Unstead, is renowned as 'the young reader's historian'. He wrote his first book, *Looking at History*, when he was the headmaster of a school in Hertfordshire.

The artist, Victor Ambrus, has illustrated many books for children and has been awarded the Kate Greenaway Medal of the Library Association.

3 cde

THE STORY OF BRITAIN: FROM WILLIAM OF ORANGE TO WORLD WAR II

R. J. UNSTEAD

THE STORY OF BRITAIN: FROM WILLIAM OF ORANGE TO WORLD WAR II

Illustrated by Victor Ambrus

A Carousel Book
TRANSWORLD PUBLISHERS LTD

THE STORY OF BRITAIN: FROM WILLIAM OF ORANGE TO WORLD WAR II

A CAROUSEL BOOK o 552 54004 8

Originally published in Great Britain by Adam and
Charles Black Ltd.

PRINTING HISTORY
Adam and Charles Black edition (one volume entitled
The Story of Britain, which forms the Carousel edition
of *The Story of Britain: From William of Orange to World
War II* and the companion Carousel volumes *The Story of
Britain: Before the Norman Conquest, In the Middle Ages*
and *In Tudor and Stuart Times*) published 1969

Carousel edition published 1971
Carousel edition reprinted 1971
Carousel edition reprinted 1972
Carousel edition reprinted 1977
Carousel edition reprinted 1984

This book is set in Intertype Baskerville

Carousel Books are published by
Transworld Publishers Ltd.,
Century House, 61–63 Uxbridge Road,
Ealing, London W5 5SA
Printed and bound in Great Britain by
Cox & Wyman Ltd., Reading, Berks.

CONTENTS

WILLIAM AND MARY

ALTHOUGH William of Orange's mother was an English princess and he had married James II's daughter, the Dutchman did not like England and had no wish to become its King. He agreed to come only because he wanted to save his beloved Holland from Louis XIV, and when he found that the English Parliament expected him to be lower than his wife, that is, to be Regent rather than King, he offered to go home again. At this, Parliament changed its tune and agreed to make William and Mary joint sovereigns. After his wife's death, he became William III.

Nor did the English people like 'Dutch Billy' very much. He was a thin, misshapen little man, with a dry manner and no smiles or graces. However, he needed England's help and England wanted a Protestant on the throne. So they made the best of each other, and in time people came to respect William's courage and unflagging spirit.

In the more distant parts of Britain, support for James II was not dead and William had to deal with risings in Scotland and Ireland. He sent an army, under General Mackay, to attack Graham of Claverhouse, now Viscount Dundee, who had raised the Highlanders for King James. In the Pass of Killiecrankie, the half-naked clansmen routed the regular troops with one murderous charge, but their victory was useless, for a bullet killed Dundee and, without a leader, they soon drifted away to their glens.

Meanwhile, James II had arrived in Ireland with money and arms provided by Louis XIV. The Irish, ready to help James in order to get rid of their Protestant landlords, laid siege to Londonderry where the Protestant inhabitants, faced by certain death if they surrendered, held out desperately for 105 days. At this point, William himself landed and marched towards Dublin. James had drawn up his army along the bank of the river Boyne but, throwing caution aside, William ordered his troops to ford the river and attack. They did so with such spirit that James again lost his nerve and galloped away to take ship to France. Southern Ireland was subdued and peace was made on the understanding that the Irish Catholics should have decent liberty, but once they had laid down their arms they were treated as harshly as ever.

In Scotland, the government declared a pardon for all who had fought in the recent rising if they would take an oath of loyalty to King William. All the chiefs took the oath except MacIan, chief of the Macdonalds at Glencoe. He delayed for as long as possible and did not arrive at Fort William until the very last day, only to find that there was no one there to accept his oath. Ham-

pered by snow, he made his way to the next town and
took the oath six days late; however, he had obeyed the
law and he went home satisfied that all was well.

But Sir John Dalrymple, the Master of Stair, hated
the Macdonalds, 'that sect of thieves' he called them,
and so did the Campbells. As the King's adviser, Dalrymple obtained permission to punish the chief for his
delay and for this purpose he sent a force of 120 Campbells to Glencoe. With Highland courtesy, the old chief
quartered his visitors as comfortably as possible in the
cottages scattered up and down the glen. For more than
a week, all was friendliness and good humour until the
fatal morning when the Campbells rose early and
slaughtered their hosts, killing them as they slept and
shooting down those who tried to escape to the snow-
bound hills.

This crime was pinned upon William by his enemies.
Certainly, he signed the order to punish the Macdonalds
but it was doubtful if he understood what Dalrymple
meant to do. What was certain was that the massacre of
Glencoe kept alive the Highlanders' hatred of the English government.

William, however, was less concerned with the puzz-
ling behaviour of his British subjects than with Louis
XIV's designs. Helped by the English fleet, he beat him
at sea and fought him on land in the Netherlands where,
in a long drawn-out war of sieges and retreats, neither
side gained much advantage. Louis' colossal extrava-
gance was ruining France and he was glad to make
peace for a time.

William was well satisfied to have saved Holland
until, quite suddenly, all his life's work seemed to be
ruined. The King of Spain was dying and Louis XIV's
grandson appeared likely to gain the throne and all the
Spanish possessions. France and Spain united would

dominate Europe, and if this should happen Holland and England were doomed. William was preparing to fight again when his horse stumbled and threw him from the saddle. His injuries, trifling to a stronger man, proved too much for a frail body weakened by ceaseless work and campaigning. He died and was succeeded by his wife's sister, Anne.

QUEEN ANNE

QUEEN ANNE was an amiable woman whose dull-witted husband, George of Denmark, played no part in British affairs, so that she was entirely under the influence of Sarah Churchill, Duchess of Marlborough. The masterful Sarah saw to it that her husband was made commander of the army, and between them they practically ruled the country.

Fortunately, Marlborough was a great soldier, probably the greatest in Britain's history. Ambitious for fame and wealth, he was also charming and patient with his difficult Dutch allies and, rare in those days, he cared for his men, saw to their food and pay and lived with them so plainly on campaign that, in affection, they called him 'Corporal John'. At first, his difficulties were immense. The British and Dutch armies were small, the Dutch rulers constantly interfered and his German and Austrian allies were proud and quarrelsome. However, having forced back the French in the Netherlands, Marlborough made a lightning move into Austria to save Vienna.

At Blenheim, he found the French and Bavarian army in a strong position, but declaring, 'I rely on the bravery and discipline of my troops,' he won a victory so complete that it changed the course of the war.

A further series of victories reduced the spirit of the French soldiers until, at the mere mention of Marlborough's name, they felt that defeat was certain. France was beaten almost to her knees and old Louis XIV was appealing with pathetic dignity to his people

to defend their own soil when Marlborough, the general who never lost a battle or failed to take a fortress, was dismissed from his command in disgrace.

He had always had enemies who resented his success and Sarah's influence but, although they put round stories that he enriched himself out of the money meant for the soldiers, they could do nothing as long as the Duchess controlled the Queen. But Anne had at last grown tired of Sarah's tantrums and she began to listen instead to the soothing voice of Mrs Masham, a lady whose Tory friends hated the great general. After a furious quarrel, the Queen plucked up courage to dismiss Sarah from the court. Marlborough's fall followed and the war with France was speedily brought to an end.

Britain gained Gibraltar, part of Canada and a good deal of respect and dislike abroad. Holland, weakened by the long war, kept her freedom and France remained too exhausted to trouble the rest of Europe for the next quarter of a century.

The most important event of Queen Anne's reign at home was the Union with Scotland. Although the two countries had had the same King since the accession of James I and VI, Scotland had kept her separate Parliament, Church and trade. It was a trading disaster that actually hastened the Union, for the Scots put a great deal of money into the Darien Scheme, an ambitious plan to make the Isthmus of Darien (Panama) into the trading centre of the world. The scheme failed and the Scots, sore about their losses, were inclined to put the blame upon the greedy English who not only kept their own trade to themselves, but had done their best to ruin their neighbours' venture. However, when tempers had cooled, it was agreed that while Scotland kept her own Church and law courts, the two countries should have one Parliament, equal trading rights and the same coinage and weights and measures. The United Kingdom of Great Britain came into existence in 1707.

Queen Anne had a very large family but all her chil-

dren died in infancy. As she grew older, she became ill
and low-spirited. It seemed to her as if God had punished her for deserting her father and she hoped that her
half-brother James Edward Stuart would come to the
throne. Parliament and a majority of the people were
totally opposed to a Catholic King, and when they found
that James refused to change his religion, they began to
look elsewhere for a Protestant monarch. They found
one in Germany where George, the grandson of Elizabeth, 'the Winter Queen', James I's daughter, was
ruling the small kingdom or electorate of Hanover.
George knew next to nothing about England but he *was*
a Protestant. To keep the Stuarts out, Parliament
invited him to accept the crown and although some of
Anne's friends still hoped to bring in James Stuart, the
Queen's sudden death upset their plans. At once, the
Elector of Hanover was proclaimed King George I.

HANOVER AND STUART

FROM the moment of George I's arrival, it was obvious that Parliament would rule the country. A German king who spoke no English could not have interfered if he had wanted to, and George soon gave up attending meetings of the council. For his part, the English were welcome to get on with their own affairs. He much preferred Hanover where the docile people did as they were told and he went back there as often as possible. George was a stout, plain man with a good deal of common sense but no charm or majesty. He was known to hate his eldest son and to have shut his own wife up in a castle for life and there was little about him or any of the Hanoverians to arouse the people's affection. For the next hundred years, the royal family was generally unpopular.

Almost at once the Jacobites, as the Stuart supporters were called, tried to recover the throne. In 1715 the Earl of Mar invited a number of Highland lords to a hunting-party which in reality was a gathering of the clans. The Standard of James VIII, 'the Pretender', was raised and from the north of England a smaller force of Jacobites, wearing the white cockade in their caps, moved towards the border.

If Mar had been anything of a general, he could have easily taken Edinburgh but 'Bobbing John' had no notion of how to lead an army. He gave the government's troops, under Argyll, plenty of time to oppose him and when they met at Sheriffmuir, the battle was so half-hearted that neither side knew which had won. As a scornful jingle expressed it:

> 'We ran and they ran, they ran and we ran,
> And we ran and they ran awa', man!'

James Edward Stuart arrived late from France bringing no help because Louis XIV had died, and in any case his mournful expression did nothing to fire his supporters' hearts. The 'Fifteen' rising collapsed and the Pretender, taking Mar with him, slunk miserably back into exile. Lack of preparation and want of courage at the top had ruined the Stuart cause. When the next chance came, it was too late. By then Sir Robert Walpole had done his work.

Walpole was a wealthy landowner from Norfolk who became the country's chief minister during George I's reign. In fact, he was Britain's first Prime Minister, though that name was not yet in use. Stout, red-faced and jovial, Walpole believed that peace and quiet were better for the country than war. So he kept taxes low, encouraged manufacture and trade, and craftily smoothed away troubles whenever they arose. 'Let sleeping dogs lie,' was his answer to all problems and, under his rule, the country had twenty years of peace.

George II, who succeeded his father in 1727, heartily disliked Walpole, but Queen Caroline, far cleverer than her husband, persuaded him to keep the Norfolk squire in power. But as time went by the old fox became unpopular. By cunning and bribery he kept control of everything in his own hands and some of the younger men felt that he cared nothing for their ability. Moreover, the nation was bored by peace and when a quarrel broke out with Spain, and a certain Captain Jenkins claimed to have had one of his ears cut off by a Spaniard, the people clamoured for war. At its outbreak they rang the church bells as though victory had already arrived. 'They are ringing the bells now,' remarked Walpole drily, 'but they soon will be wringing their hands.'

The war went badly, partly because Walpole himself had neglected to spend money on the navy and the army. Britain found herself fighting for Queen Maria Theresa of Austria against France and Spain and, on the continent, George II himself led an army to protect his cherished Hanover. At Dettingen, the last battle in which a British King took the field, a lively horse carried him towards the rear but, dismounting, he stoutly declared that he would fight on foot since his legs would never run away. Sword in hand and roaring, 'Steady, my brave boys, steady!' he brought his troops to victory.

Shortly afterwards, however, his son, the Duke of Cumberland, was defeated by the French at Fontenoy. At this, the spirits of the Jacobites rose, expecially as they now had an inspiring leader in Charles Edward, the handsome son of the Old Pretender.

Unfortunately for his hopes, a French invasion fleet was scattered by storms, and after this the French decided that the Scottish and English Jacobites were too weak to be worth helping. So when Charles Edward landed in Scotland to win back his father's kingdom, he was accompanied by only seven friends. Without large-scale French help, it was madness to attempt an uprising and the Prince received a cool reception from the Scottish chieftains.

But Charles Edward did not appeal to common sense. In the name of honour and loyalty, he asked the clansmen to follow him and they could not refuse. When Cameron of Lochiel spoke of his doubts, Charles Edward retorted, 'Lochiel may stay at home and learn his Prince's fate from the newspapers.'

'Not so,' cried Lochiel, 'if you are resolved on that rash undertaking, I will go with you!'

Within days, over two thousand Highlanders had joined the Jacobite army which moved to Perth and on to Edinburgh where the Old Pretender was proclaimed King. A small force under General Cope was easily routed at Prestonpans and, for the next six weeks, Bonnie Prince Charlie held court at Holyrood winning the hearts of all who met him, but waiting in vain for news of a general uprising in his favour. Worse, the delay gave the government time to bring Cumberland and his army back from the continent.

At length, in November, 1745, the march on England began. Taking the westward route to avoid an English army at Newcastle, Charles captured Carlisle and entered Lancashire with an army of about 5,000. The English Jacobites did not stir. Thirty years had passed since the last Stuart fiasco and under Walpole's comfortable rule, they had learned to put up with the Hanoverians. On December 4th, when Charles Edward reached

Derby, only 130 miles from London, his discouraged chieftains refused to march another step. Their men were already beginning to slip away and two English armies lay between them and home. It was madness to go on. But at this stage it was probably folly to go back. They did not know that London was in a panic and King George was making ready to leave. Anything could have happened if they had gone on, but on 'Black Friday' they turned about and began the long march back. Charles, who had formerly marched gaily with the troops, now rode in dejected silence.

Cumberland was presently at their heels but Lord George Murray beat him off and the Prince and his army reached Glasgow after marching six hundred miles in less than two months. They defeated a royal army at Falkirk but instead of capturing Stirling Castle, Charles was persuaded to retire into the Highlands. Cumberland came on remorselessly. At Culloden Moor, near Inverness, he at last caught up with the Jacobite army and although the Highlanders fought with all their desperate valour, they were utterly defeated. Two officers seized Charles's bridle and forced him from the field and Cumberland was left to crush resistance with such blood-thirsty cruelty that he earned the name of 'Butcher'.

With a price of £30,000 upon his head, Charles wandered about the Highlands and the Western Isles for five months, hunted by the government troops but protected by the loyalty of people to whom thirty guineas would have been a fortune. Not one betrayed him. In caves and huts, they fed and clothed him and led him by secret paths to fresh hiding-places.

Once, when capture seemed certain, a lady named Flora MacDonald brought him a dress in order to disguise him as 'Betty Burke', her Irish maid, and, although the tall 'maid' took overlong strides and managed her skirts clumsily, Flora succeeded in taking the Prince past the soldiers to another island.

At last a boat was found to carry the gallant youth away to France. He never returned to Scotland. Many years later, when an unhappy old drunkard named Charles Edward Stuart died in Rome, his name was forgotten and unmourned except in Scotland. There they still cherished the pattern of Betty Burke's dress and sang of that brave lad 'born to be King'. But the Jacobite cause was dead.

RISE OF AN EMPIRE

FOR more than a century, despite all the troubles at home, Britain – and England in particular – had been getting richer. Trade produced bigger and quicker profits than farming or manufactures, and more English ships put out to sea for lawful trade than for the old-style piracy. There were still expeditions to the Spanish Main but men like William Dampier who lived for years among the buccaneers and ended by becoming a celebrated navigator, tended to become merchant captains rather than sea-robbers. They could find employment with various enterprises such as the African Company, the Levant Company in the Mediterranean, the Hudson Bay Company and the rich East India Company. There were sugar plantations in Barbados which produced more wealth than all the North American colonies, fisheries off Newfoundland and the Baltic trade in rope, timber and tallow. As the profits came home to the rich merchants and were spread out to lesser businessmen and tradesmen, England took on a more gracious, prosperous air.

Trade had to be fought for and protected. The Forty-five Rebellion was only a part of the wider struggle into which Britain was drawn. The wars on the continent between Frederick the Great of Prussia and most of the rest of Europe did not interest the British government very much, apart from the King's nervousness for Hanover.

But across the oceans were matters of great importance. The Spaniards were still trying to keep all the South American trade to themselves, and the French plan to link their colony in Canada to Louisiana in the south was a threat to the English colonies along the coast of North America. Since Captain John Smith's time, more than a million settlers had made their homes there and as they pushed inland, building villages and clearing the woods for farms, they found that the French, often in alliance with the Red Indians, were their enemies.

In India there was much fiercer rivalry. For over a century the East India Company had been sending home cargoes of luxuries, and there were French merchants engaged in the same profitable business. The country itself had fallen into disorder. There was no strong government but a number of Indian princes constantly at war with each other. The Europeans therefore built forts and enlisted local troops to protect their warehouses and an English or a French governor, with a few disciplined troops under European officers, could become extremely powerful by aiding one prince against another. It was clear that if one side ousted the other, the victor would possess the richest trade in the world.

For a time the French made much better progress. With a clever governor named Dupleix, they gained

control of most of southern India and were on the point of putting an end to English influence when a harum-scarum clerk, who had recently taken to soldiering, changed the situation.

Robert Clive was taken prisoner when the French captured Madras, but having escaped by disguising himself as an Indian, he joined the East India Company's force and volunteered to attack Arcot, capital of the French-controlled province. He expected that this would draw off a huge army which was besieging Trichinopoly, the last town in which the British had some interest. His daring plan succeeded. With only 200 European troops and about 300 Indian sepoys, he took Arcot and held its crumbling walls for fifty days against an army of 10,000. British prestige was saved. The prince whom they supported ousted the French candidate and Dupleix was sent home in disgrace. Clive, no longer the black sheep of his family, returned to England with a fortune.

When the Seven Years War broke out in 1756, Britain was seen to be hard-pressed everywhere – in Europe, in

North America and in India. Admiral Byng was executed on his own quarter-deck for failing to recapture the
island of Minorca, the Duke of Cumberland surrendered
an army on the continent; Frederick the Great, now
Britain's ally, was severely defeated several times and
the French general, Montcalm, appeared certain to
secure the whole of Canada. These disasters brought to
power William Pitt, a country gentleman who had long
been prominent in Parliament as a sarcastic critic of the
government and the King. George II detested Pitt but
he had to accept him as his chief minister, for Pitt, 'that
terrible cornet of horse', was very popular in the country
and had enormous confidence in himself. 'I know I can
save this country,' he declared, 'and no one else can!'

With energy and boldness, he attacked France so that
she never knew where the next blow would fall, supplied
Frederick the Great with gold to keep his armies in the
field, strengthened the British forces on the continent
and used the navy to support operations all over the
world. Above all, he had the gift of choosing good commanders and of inspiring men with his own determination. 'No man,' it was said, 'ever entered his room who
did not feel himself braver at his return than when he
went in.'

Clive had already returned to India when Sarajah
Dowlah, a young prince who favoured the French, captured the English trading-post at Calcutta. One hundred
and forty-six prisoners were crammed into a tiny room
where all but twenty-three died from thirst and
suffocation during a single night. News of this incident,
the Black Hole of Calcutta, brought Clive up from
Madras to recapture the trading-post. The 'heaven-born
general', as Pitt called him, then decided to depose Sarajah Dowlah in order to prevent the French taking control of Bengal, a province larger than Great Britain

itself. With a tiny force, he completely routed Dowlah's vast army at the battle of Plassey and in the next three years, aided by Colonel Eyre Coote's fighting regiments and an efficient naval squadron working off the coasts, he destroyed all traces of French influence in India.

THE TAKING OF QUEBEC

ONE of several officers brought to Pitt's notice at this
time was James Wolfe, a thin red-haired youngster with
a sloping chin and little of the soldier's military bearing.
However, Wolfe had fought at Dettingen and Culloden
and had distinguished himself in raids upon the French
coast, besides offending some of his senior officers by his
unmannerly remarks about the feeble way in which the
army was run. When Pitt had him promoted to general
and sent to attack the great French port of Louisbourg
in America, they complained to George II that Wolfe

was mad. The fellow read books and poetry, they said, and he had no respect for his seniors:

'Mad, is he?' growled the old King. 'Then I hope he will bite some others of my generals!'

Wolfe captured Louisbourg, and was ordered to take Quebec, the fortress-town which the French had built on the St Lawrence River. Situated high above the river and strongly defended by more than a hundred guns and by Montcalm's army, the town appeared to be untakable. From their lofty position, the French disdainfully watched the British landing troops on the bank of the river. No army would ever scale their cliffs and, in any case, the Canadian winter would force the enemy to retire. With first-class service from Admiral Saunders, Wolfe got guns and men up the river; he bombarded Quebec and made an unsuccessful attack upon Montcalm's outlying camp but there seemed to be no prospect of getting near to the town, let alone of capturing it.

As summer wore on, Wolfe fell ill and by the time he had hit upon a plan, he was so weak that he had to beg the army doctor to merely 'patch' him up and kill his pain for a few days. He broke camp, moved troops up and down the river to make the French doubtful of his intentions and had the warships open an all-night bombardment of the town. In the darkness, he landed with 1,700 picked men at a tiny cove at the foot of the cliffs where he had seen women of Quebec washing their clothes in the river. With a spy-glass, he had picked out the zig-zag path which they used and it was on this path that he based his hopes.

A party of volunteers hauled themselves up the cliff, overpowered the guard at the top and signalled to their companions to follow. More boats drifted down river and by dawn Wolfe had an army of 4,500 men with two field-guns drawn up on the Plains of Abraham, a mile or so from Quebec. Deciding to act before the British could bring up reinforcements, Montcalm hastily formed his men into columns of attack and led them against the enemy. On Wolfe's order, the British held their fire until the French were within forty paces of their ranks. The volley burst out and under cover of the smoke, the British reloaded, advanced twenty paces and fired again. Then they charged. Within moments, the battle had become a rout and the French army had fled, save here and there, where their white-coated regulars fought to the end. By then, Wolfe was dead and Montcalm was dying of his wounds.

The sharp-shooters had marked Wolfe's bright new uniform and he was hit early on but he somehow gave the order to charge: 'Hold me up!' he muttered to an officer. 'They must not see me fall!' The soldiers advanced and he heard shouts and cheers. Someone told him the French were on the run. He raised himself and gave orders to cut off their retreat. He knew that his gamble had succeeded; Quebec and Canada, too, would be taken by the British. 'I die content,' he whispered. As Pitt said later, he died in the moment when his fame began.

In that same year, 1759, when Quebec was captured and the news of Plassey arrived, English regiments helped to win a victory at Minden which saved Frederick the Great; Admiral Boscawen beat one French fleet at sea and Admiral Hawke destroyed another in Quiberon Bay to put an end to the threat of invasion. This was the Year of Victories when people said that the church bells were wearing out from so much joyous pealing.

It was also the high-water mark of Pitt's success for, in the following year, George II died and his son, George

III, was soon able to bring the war to an end. He wanted to be rid of Pitt and to have his own friends in power. It was clear that Britain had made enormous gains from the war and was now supreme in trade and upon the seas. But Frederick the Great felt left in the lurch by his ally and he never forgave George III's treachery. As for Pitt, he took the title of Earl of Chatham and retired to his country house, growling angrily about the terms of the peace.

THE NAVY AND CAPTAIN COOK

THE Royal Navy, on which Britain's power rested for the next 150 years, had known many ups and downs since Henry VIII's reign. It fell into ruins and was rebuilt by Sir John Hawkins for Queen Elizabeth, who could also call upon large numbers of armed merchantmen and privateers when danger was at hand. Peace with Spain and Charles I's money difficulties again reduced the fleet to a sorry state and although there was a revival in Cromwell's time, the Dutch War in Charles II's reign revealed the helplessness of an island that neglected its navy.

The weakness was not solely due to dishonesty and neglect. Officers were part-timers, posted to a ship, as a rule, when war broke out and likely to return to private life after the danger had passed. Some were court favourites who, finding it fashionable to 'serve a commission' against the Dutch, obtained command of a ship

without much experience of the sea or any intention of
making the navy their career. Needless to say, these
'fair-weather officers' were not liked by the 'tarpaulin'
captains, men of little polish or education who had
served in ships since their boyhood days. In Charles II's
reign, Samuel Pepys, Secretary of the Admiralty, de-
voted his life to correcting this state of affairs and it was
due to his efforts that the navy came to have trained
officers who had passed examinations in seamanship.

Thus, by the time of the Georges, the navy had
become a regular, instead of a part-time, career. The
seamen were little changed; they were still merchant
sailors and fishermen who joined or were forced to serve
in the royal ships. The admirals were still mostly from
noble families but those in the next grade, the captains,
had come up from the bottom, starting as a rule as mid-
shipmen, and earning their promotion the hard way.
Most of them were sons of lesser gentry and because the
favour of a high-placed relative was useful, they usually
rose more easily than the few who came up from the
lower deck or from the merchant service. However, they
were all trained, professional sailors.

A notable episode in the navy's development was
Anson's voyage round the world. In 1740 Captain
George Anson was dispatched with six ships to 'vex' the
Spaniards in the Pacific. He carried out his orders perfectly, capturing a port and a huge treasure galleon and
playing havoc with Spanish trade. Then, like Drake, he
crossed the Pacific and came home via the Cape, having
survived countless dangers and the loss of 626 of his 961
men in the first year of the four-year voyage. His superb
leadership produced results far greater than the treasure
on board the *Centurion*. Anson was promoted to
admiral and in time at least eight of the junior officers
who served under him also reached admiral's rank, so

that the experience and inspiration of that great voyage
provided a lasting tradition in the navy.

Admiral Saunders, who carried General Wolfe and
his army to Quebec, had been one of Anson's officers and
when the fleet reached the St Lawrence, Saunders chose
a quiet Yorkshireman named Cook to sail ahead in the
Mercury to make charts of the river's shoals and sand-
banks. Cook carried out his task so well that, to the as-
tonishment of the French, the British fleet was able to
drop anchor below Quebec without losing a single
vessel.

James Cook had earned his first pennies scaring crows
but, at fifteen, he was at sea in a Whitby collier engaged
in carrying coal down the coast to London. His master
taught the serious-minded apprentice all he knew of
navigation and Cook had become mate of the collier,
when he decided to enlist in the navy as an able seaman.
He rose slowly, for he had no advantages of birth or

education, but his outstanding abilities had already been noticed when he was chosen to chart the St Lawrence.

Nine years later, when the Admiralty proposed to send a ship to the Pacific to study the path of the planet Venus and to make reports upon the geography, people and botany of that vast area, Lieutenant Cook was given command of the *Endeavour*. With a crew of eighty-five, some scientists and artists, he rounded Cape Horn and reached the island of Tahiti where the scientists pursued their observations, and the sailors made friends with the easy-going natives.

Cook then sailed into almost unknown seas. A continent called Terra Australis was supposed to lie to the south; a Dutchman named Tasman had brought home some vague reports and William Dampier had reached Western Australia. Lack of water had forced Dampier to depart and no one knew the size or extent of this

southern land nor anything about the thousands of islands scattered in the ocean. The *Endeavour* reached New Zealand which was found to consist of two islands, inhabited by the fierce Maoris. Having made careful charts, Cook sailed on to Australia where he explored the east coast for 2,000 miles and almost lost his ship on the Barrier Reef before returning to England.

The voyage had taken three years and thirty out of the crew of eighty-five had died, mostly from scurvy, so when Cook, promoted to the rank of captain, sailed again, he made sure that his men ate less salt meat than usual but far more fruit and vegetables than they liked. A sailor who disobeyed him was given a dozen lashes, but at the end of the second voyage which also lasted three years and took the *Resolution* far into the icy waters of the Antarctic, only one man out of 118 had died of sickness.

For his third voyage as a commander, Cook again chose the sturdy *Resolution* and he was accompanied by a second vessel, the *Discovery*. This was to be an even more extensive voyage of exploration, not only of the South Pacific but of the Arctic Ocean in search of the North-West Passage. When no trace of a way to the Atlantic could be found, the ships headed south again to cruise among the islands where Cook and his sailors were by now well-known to the natives.

At Hawaii, where Cook was regarded as a god-like person, the natives were as friendly as ever but their habit of stealing anything they fancied caused a good deal of annoyance. One day, Cook went ashore with a small party of marines to talk to a friendly old chief about the theft of one of the ship's boats. He invited him to accompany him back on board, probably hoping to detain him there until the mssing boat was returned. The chief cheerfully agreed but on the way to the beach, his wives and relatives became alarmed and set up a loud wailing. This brought an excited crowd to the scene and by the time Cook and his companions had reached the water's edge, they were so closely pressed that the marines could not have used their weapons. Seeing this, a boat-party, just off-shore, fired some warning shots, upon which Cook, who had kept perfectly calm, turned and called out to the boats to cease firing. As he turned, he was stabbed in the back and quickly clubbed to death in the shallow water.

Thus, on his third great voyage, Cook was killed in a petty squabble by the people whom he had always treated with kindness and understanding. He was one of the world's most notable discoverers, a leader and a man of noble character.

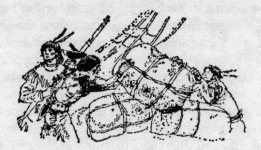

THE AMERICAN COLONIES

WHILE Cook was voyaging in the South Seas there occurred in North America a dispute so ill-tempered that it led to a war and to the rise of a new nation.

By this time, the American settlers numbered more than two million and nearly all of them or their fathers had crossed the ocean because they had been unhappy or oppressed at home. By hard toil they had built homes and businesses and it was not surprising that many of them, especially in the Puritan colonies of New England, felt no love for Britain. They grumbled about the law which forbade them to trade with any other country and they disliked the haughty officials who came out to manage their affairs and to accuse them of smuggling when they did undercover business with the French and the Dutch. Nor did they feel any gratitude for the armed protection they had been given in the recent wars and they saw no reason to pay for the soldiers who were defending their frontiers against the Red Indians.

George III, a pleasant, stupid young man, was determined to play a bigger part in his country's affairs than George I or George II had done. Remembering his mother's advice to 'be a king', he managed to build up a party of 'King's Friends' in Parliament so that he could rule through ministers of his own choosing. Unfortunately, he chose men not for their cleverness but for their willingness to please him and Pitt was now too old and ill to oppose him.

Thus, when George and his ministers decided that the colonies should pay part of the cost of their own defence, the matter was handled badly.

The government put taxes on a few articles such as glass, paper and tea, and the colonists refused to pay. They raised the cry of 'No taxation without representation', meaning that it was not fair for them to have to pay taxes ordered by Parliament at Westminster where they had no members. Pitt came out of retirement to support them and all the taxes were taken off except the one on tea.

By a special arrangement, tea was actually cheaper than before but a party of indignant colonists, dressed as Red Indians, boarded three ships in Boston harbour and threw their cargoes of tea into the water.

It was the King's turn to get angry, and after the Boston Tea Party his minister, Lord North, punished the colony by closing the port. At this, the colonists drew up a petition to the King, setting out their grievances but also stating their loyalty to the crown. George III ignored the petition.

Fighting broke out in New England, when a force of British soldiers was sent to seize a store of arms at Lexington. As they marched inland, the redcoats were sniped at from the woods by 'Minute men', so-called because they were ready to turn out at a minute's notice. Then came the battle of Bunker's Hill. This piece of high land overlooking Boston harbour had been occupied by the local citizen-soldiers who were only driven off after the

regular troops had suffered heavy casualties. The War of
American Independence had begun.

Having blundered into war, George III and his ministers appeared to have no idea how to win it. Their red-
coated soldiers, many of them hired from Germany,
were commanded by officers who were baffled by an
enemy who refused to fight European-style battles but
preferred to use their knowledge of a vast wooded
country in order to ambush and harass the regulars. In
any case, the British commanders felt that they had
merely to sit still and wait for the opposition to collapse.
The Colonists lacked artillery and warships; they were
ill-equipped, quarrelsome and at times even treach-
erous, so that a commander like Wolfe or Clive would
have speedily brought the war to an end. However, there
was no plan of action but only confusing orders from
London, and the colonists were held together by their
commander-in-chief, George Washington, a man of
superb tenacity and courage. At length, after three years
spent 'in teaching the Americans how to fight', the
British suffered a major reverse when General Bur-
goyne's army of 8,000 men was surrounded and captured at Saratoga.

In a European campaign the surrender of one small
army would not have mattered very much but in America it lost the war. Britain's enemies could see that the
colonists had a chance of victory and France and Spain
entered the war. Holland joined them and most of the
other countries of Europe agreed to defy the British
navy's practice of searching neutral ships for cargoes
intended for America. When foreign warships arrived in
American waters, the Royal Navy was outnumbered
and this temporary loss of sea-power was decisive. Lord
Cornwallis, commanding a British army at Yorktown,
was in no particular danger from George Washington's

forces until a French fleet appeared off the coast. This completely changed the situation and Cornwallis was compelled to surrender.

'O God! It is all over!' cried Lord North when he heard the news. This was true, for although Admiral Rodney regained command of the sea by defeating the French and Spanish fleets near some islands called the Saints, his victory came too late. Britain had to recognize the independence of the American colonies in order to deal with her other enemies. Despite having been bested by a few thousand armed settlers, Britain fended off France and Spain without great difficulty and when peace was made, the only important losses were the thirteen American colonies and Minorca. Canada, India and Gibraltar, all threatened during the war, remained in the empire.

INVENTORS AND ENGINEERS

GEORGE III's failure in America put an end to his ambition to 'be a king' and his opponents, the Whigs, took over the government. However, when they proved to be as selfish and greedy as the ministers whom they had attacked, George III took a daring step to get rid of them. As First Lord of the Treasury or prime minister, he appointed William Pitt, son of Pitt the elder. Pitt was only twenty-four. He was an earnest, unsmiling young man who had studied hard to follow in his father's steps, but he had few supporters in the House of Commons and the Whigs declared it was ridiculous to put the country's government into the hands of anyone so young. It was, they said:

> 'A sight to make surrounding nations stare,
> A kingdom trusted to a schoolboy's care.'

But the 'schoolboy' had the people's support. They remembered how old Pitt had saved the country and they gave his son the chance to prove himself. For the next twenty years, Pitt the Younger remained prime minister. Scorning to enrich himself as many other politicians had done, he insisted that officials should be more honest and hardworking than in the past and he did much to encourage trade and manufacture.

Until the eighteenth century the country's prosperity rested mainly on farming and sea-trade. Manufacturing, even of cloth, was mostly carried on at home and in small workshops; coal was little used except in

44

household grates and two-thirds of all the iron came from abroad. Then there arose a group of inventors whose ideas made Britain into the chief manufacturing country in the world.

A Lancashire man named James Kay invented a shuttle which, by means of springs, returned to the weaver's right hand, leaving his left hand free to operate a bar or batten. The Flying Shuttle speeded up weaving so much that faster spinning was required and James Hargreaves, a poor cottager, realized how this could be done when he saw his wife's spinning wheel fall over and continue to spin on its side. His *Spinning Jenny* with its upright spindles was further improved by Richard Arkwright, a barber whose journeys to buy human hair for wig-making took him into the cottages of Lancashire cloth-workers. His inventive mind was fascinated by the problem of how to produce thread still faster for the weavers, and with the help of a clockmaker he began to experiment. The work had to be carried out in secret because the workers feared that machines would put an end to their own jobs, but after many setbacks, the partners succeeded in producing an efficient spinning-frame.

Arkwright's machines were driven by water-power, which meant that workers had to work together in mills or factories built near streams. When Samuel Crompton used the ideas of earlier inventors to produce an improved machine called a *Mule*, spinning became so quick that it was the turn of the weavers to cry out for better looms. Power, more reliable than water, was needed. For many years, steam-engines invented by Thomas Newcomen, had been used to pump water out of shallow mines, but they were clumsy machines requiring a great deal of fuel to produce a small amount of power. One day, early in the reign of George III, a model of Newcomen's engine was sent for repair to an instrument-maker at Glasgow University named James Watt. This brilliant Scot discovered how the engine's faults might be overcome but he could not have produced a successful steam-engine without the patient help of Matthew Boulton, owner of a Birmingham engineering works, who became his partner. Together, they turned out hundreds of steam-engines to pump water and to drive machines of every kind, including the power-looms invented by the Reverend Cartwright.

Steam-power created a new world of machines and factories, of skilled engineers, mechanics and ill-paid workers. Difficulties of all kinds had to be overcome. The engineers were hampered by a shortage of iron but as charcoal gave way to coal for smelting, the iron industry moved north where ironmasters, like John 'Iron Mad' Wilkinson, produced the enormous quantities of metal which the surging industries demanded.

Another difficulty was the state of the roads. To move heavy loads of materials by wagon was a slow and costly business but when James Brindley, an uneducated genius, built the Worsley Canal for the Duke of Bridgewater, the price of coal in Manchester fell by half. This led to the building of canals to link the navigable rivers to the factory and mining areas.

In barely fifty years, large parts of Britain were transformed. The bleak moors and quiet valleys of Yorkshire, Lancashire, South Wales and Lanarkshire became crowded with manufacturing and mining villages where the workers, drawn in from the countryside, came to live in buildings flung up as cheaply and quickly as possible, usually without sanitation, comfort or any of the decencies of life. It was a harsh and brutal age, but it was also an age of elegance and opportunity. While the rich, many of whom had recently won their wealth in India or in the new industries, could enjoy luxury in its most gracious forms, the poorest classes lived in brutish squalor. But, bad as the contrast was between England's rich and poor, it was mild compared with conditions in France.

TRAFALGAR

IN France, apparently so powerful and rich, the peasants suffered monstrous oppression in order to support the most splendid and most idle aristocracy in the world. Despite its magnificence, the country was almost bankrupt and the workers were near starvation. A food riot in Paris grew into a revolution and Louis XVI, a harmless simpleton, and his unpopular wife, Marie Antoinette, were executed, along with hundreds of aristocrats who had failed to flee abroad.

Those who believed in liberty and justice were thrust aside by the leaders of the blood-thirsty Paris mob. Appalling crimes took place and government, snatched by one or another group of petty villains, fell into ruin while the ragged armies of France repelled its enemies along the frontiers. The European powers, notably Austria, Prussia and Great Britain, had little sympathy for Louis XVI or for the French aristocrats in exile but the revolution alarmed them, especially when the French declared that they would help any people who rose against their rulers.

War broke out and it was during a British naval

attack on Toulon that the port was saved by a young artillery officer named Napoleon Bonaparte. He was a Corsican of Italian descent who had attended a French military college shortly before the revolution. War and the disappearance of most of the aristocratic officers gave him the chance to rise, and at twenty-six, Bonaparte was a general. By a series of brilliant victories in Italy, he defeated Austria and then, fired by a dream of conquering an empire in the East, he took an army to Egypt. His plans were dashed when Admiral Nelson sailed into Aboukir Bay and destroyed his fleet as it lay at anchor at the mouth of the Nile. At this reverse, Napoleon abandoned his army and returned to Paris where, with the people's acclaim, he overthrew the government and made himself absolute master of France.

As First Consul and presently as Emperor, he magically restored the fortunes of France. The swarthy little Corsican was a genius whose superhuman energy enabled him to govern the country, to win campaigns and to dominate everyone from officials and generals to kings and queens. Victory followed victory until half of Europe had been defeated in the field or cowed into submission by a dictator whose matchless armies were filled by officers chosen for their ability in battle and by soldiers who worshipped their invincible commander.

Pitt conducted the war against France in much the same style as his father had done forty years earlier, though with less energy and fire. The navy held the seas and English gold supported the armies of allies on the continent, but when these allies were beaten, all that stood between Napoleon and complete victory was the English Channel. Once across that narrow strait, the Grand Army would make short work of Britain's meagre forces.

One hundred and fifty thousand of the finest troops

in the world were assembled on the cliffs of Boulogne; the
barges and stores lay ready for the invasion and all that
was needed for complete success was a few days' control
of the Channel. To a general of Napoleon's capacity, it
would have been easy to solve such a problem on land but
the French navy was shut up in harbour and Napoleon
could only rage at his admirals' failure to move their
ships as quickly and precisely as cavalry or guns. At last,
however, Admiral Villeneuve managed to get his ships
out of Toulon harbour while the watching British squadron had been withdrawn for a refit. Nelson, furious at
having been given the slip, chased Villeneuve to the
West Indies and back across the Atlantic towards the
approaches to the Channel where the French ran into an
English squadron. Villeneuve turned away and took

refuge in Cadiz harbour. Napoleon's invasion plan was
ruined and, in disgust, he broke camp at Boulogne and
marched away to destroy the armies of Austria and
Russia at Ulm and Austerlitz. The news killed Pitt. All
his hopes had been pinned on his latest alliance and men
said the 'Austerlitz look' never left his face until his death
a few weeks later. He was only forty-six and he died in
despair, murmuring, 'My country! How I leave my
country!'

The outlook was indeed dark. The combined armies
of Europe seemed unable to withstand Napoleon whose
latest triumph, a crushing victory over the Prussians and
a treaty with the Tsar of Russia, gave him control of the
entire continent. Moreover, he intended to use this
power to kill Britain's trade by closing all the ports and

markets of Europe to her goods. This, he felt certain, would bring that 'nation of shopkeepers' to their knees.

One victory relieved the gloom. While Napoleon was beating the Austrians, his navy was destroyed at Trafalgar by Lord Nelson, the best-loved of all sea-commanders. This slight, spare man who had gone to sea from his father's Norfolk vicarage at the age of thirteen and had suffered scurvy, fever and the loss of an arm and an eye in his country's service, possessed the same kind of passionate heroism that fired James Wolfe. In him was the same contempt for senior authority, the same dedication to his profession and his men and the same resolve for a victory so complete that it would bring immortality.

After Villeneuve had escaped into Cadiz, Nelson rejoined the fleet off the coast of Spain, where he lay at a distance, concealing his strength and moving ships away in hope of enticing the enemy out. At length, one of the frigates, poised to carry news of a move, brought word that the French and Spanish ships had left harbour and were standing out to sea.

At once, Nelson ordered his fleet to carry out the prearranged plan. His captains knew what was needed and the Admiral had only to signal 'General Chase South-East' for them to take up their stations in two columns which moved slowly towards the enemy on the lightest of breezes. As they closed in, Nelson's flag-ship showed another signal, 'England Expects That Every Man This Day Will Do His Duty'.

'What is Nelson signalling about?' cried one captain. 'We all know what we have to do!' But the seamen greeted the message with cheers which rolled across the water from one ship to the next and a band played 'Britons Strike Home' as the black-and-yellow-painted three-deckers moved into a storm of fire from the strung-out French fleet. With Nelson in the *Victory* leading one column and Collingwood in the *Royal Sovereign* leading the other, they pierced the enemy line at right angles in two places, and, having done so, every ship in the British fleet, except for one or two in the rear, found an opponent for the 'pell-mell' battle which followed. At close quarters, when the great ships came alongside each other, riggings became hopelessly entangled aloft, broadsides raked the decks and boarding-parties slashed away as volleys were presented at point-blank range.

In this kind of fighting, the French were no match for their enemy's experience. In Nelson's ships, 450 men were killed but Villeneuve lost nearly 5,000; the rear and centre of his fleet were destroyed and Napoleon's navy ceased to exist.

Trafalgar was the greatest British victory of all time. It brought command of the seas for a century and made certain that Britain could not be defeated by the French Emperor. But at home the news was received with sorrow and tears. Nelson was dead. At the height of the battle, he was walking the twenty-foot length of his quarter-deck wearing a uniform coat bright with the four embroidered stars of his Orders of Knighthood, when a French sharp-shooter up on the mizzen-mast of the *Redoubtable* leaned forward and shot him at a range of only fifteen yards.

The loss of one maimed little admiral stunned the nation, for the people loved him and had already made him their national hero. His sailors, those hard-drinking ruffians, wept for him. A young sailor wrote of him to his parents, 'all the men in our ship who have seen him are such soft toads, they have done nothing but blast their eyes and cry ever since he was killed . . . Chaps that fought like the Devil sit down and cry like a wench.'

WATERLOO

IN order to make all Europe obey his order to do no trade with Britain, Napoleon drove out the royal family of Portugal and put his own brother upon the Spanish throne. This was to close the last way in for English goods, but the Portuguese and the Spaniards broke into revolt and called to Britain for help. Thanks to the navy, a small British army was landed in Portugal which became the base for the prolonged struggle known as the Peninsular War.

In command of the British force was a beak-nosed martinet whose experience of fighting on the dusty plains of India stood him in good stead in Spain's parched and mountainous countryside. He was Arthur Wellesley, later Duke of Wellington. This unbending aristocrat who regarded Nelson as a showman, his officers as dandified boobies and his men as the scum of the earth, came to Spain with one ambition – to beat the French. He knew how to do it and he had the patience to carry out his plan in the face of every difficulty. To Wellington, war was a matter of preparation and hard sense. He understood the problems. The French, led by Napoleon's best marshals, had vastly superior numbers and the confidence that victory belonged always to them. The country could barely support its poverty-stricken peasants, let alone an army on campaign. As allies, the Portuguese were brave but undisciplined and the Spaniards were useless in formal battles against the French. Defeat would result in the recall of the British troops and victory must take a long, long time to secure. In fact it took four years.

During that time Wellington crossed and recrossed Spain, beating the French in battle, drawing them after him to exhaust their supplies, falling back to the fortified lines he had constructed outside Lisbon and advancing warily back into Spain when the enemy retreated. In this drawn-out contest, he transformed his ill-conditioned troops into the finest little army in Europe. He had called them 'a rabble' and he made them into his 'fine fellows'. 'With that army, I could have done anything,' he declared. They did not love 'Old Nosey' in the way that men loved Marlborough and Nelson but they trusted him. The sight of his long nose was worth ten thousand men any day, they said.

At Vimiero, Talavera, Busaco, Albuera and Salamanca, Wellington beat the French, as he said he would. After Vitoria, he drove them out of Spain, and at Toulouse he beat them on French soil. It was after that battle that he heard the astounding news of Napoleon's abdication.

While he was abusing his marshals for their failures in Spain, Napoleon had been preparing the defeat of Russia. By 1812 he was ready, and at the head of the finest army that ever marched in column, he advanced to Moscow. The Russians fought and retreated, burning the countryside as they went. Moscow was empty. Amid the ruins, Napoleon waited for the Tsar's peace proposals but none came; there was no one to deal with, no visible army to fight and, worse still, no supplies in the capital to support his own army through the winter. As snow began to fall he gave the order to retreat from Moscow, but he was already far too late. Cold and hunger destroyed the grand Army. Out of that magnificent host, half a million strong, barely 40,000 men survived the march back. By then they were no longer recognizable as soldiers, and Napoleon had long since deserted them. He had raced ahead to raise fresh armies for, scenting his downfall, Europe was up in arms against him. He fought brilliantly but his enemies were too numerous. Paris fell and the French turned against the man who had heaped so much glory and disaster upon his adopted country. Napoleon abdicated and was sent into exile on the island of Elba.

In less than a year he escaped and returned to France. The people, already sick of defeat, welcomed him with joy and his old soldiers flocked back into the ranks. The

allies who had disbanded their forces, hastily scraped
together an army and asked Wellington to proceed to
Belgium to take command. It was a mixed collection of
troops and he regretted that most of his Peninsular vet-
erans were missing. Still, he had the Guards and some
reliable infantry and there were the Prussians some way
off, under Blücher, a tough old general whom he
trusted.

Napoleon moved north out of France and defeated
Blücher. Believing that the Prussians were done for, he
then came on to deal with Wellington, who was waiting
for him behind a ridge near the village of Waterloo.
There was a long slope up to the ridge and Wellington
garrisoned three forward positions as strong-points to
hold up the enemy.

The attack started at noon when the French made
furious assaults on the outposts and surged in columns
against the army behind the ridge. Wellington met them
as he had met them in Spain, with volleys, with British
squares and, when the opportunity arose, with the bayonet. It was desperate work, 'hard pounding', Wellington called it, 'we must see who can pound the
hardest'. He was everywhere, encouraging his tired
troops, praising the Guards, calling for one more brave
effort. Constantly, he looked for the Prussians. Blücher,
old 'Marshal Forwards', would not fail him but he
wanted him badly. In the late afternoon, a movement
was sighted away to the left. It was the Prussians.

Napoleon increased his efforts to overwhelm the
British. In four massed charges the French cavalry was
hurled against the infantry squares which held firm 'as
though rooted to earth'; the Prussians were checked and
as dusk began to fall the Imperial Guard was ordered up
the slope. With majestic calm, 6000 picked soldiers, the
very aristocrats of Napoleon's army, advanced in parade

order to the tap of the drum, their officers out in front with drawn swords. The British waited behind their ridge. At fifty paces, they stood up and fired one terrible volley. The enemy line wavered. A deep voice called out, 'Now's the time, my boys!' and the British sprang forward with the bayonet. The Imperial Guard broke and fled down the slope as the Prussians burst through on the left and the battle became a rout.

White-faced and still blaming his defeat on Marshal Ney's cavalry tactics, Napoleon got into his carriage and made for Paris. Unable to raise yet another army, he surrendered to the British from whom he expected better treatment than from the vengeful Prussians. This time there was to be no escape. Exiled to St Helena in the South Atlantic, the Corsican Emperor of France died there after six years of captivity.

THE RAILWAYS

TWENTY-FIVE years of revolution and war on the continent had made little difference to the lives of the people in Britain. They had seen nothing of the enemy or of the violent overthrow of governments and ruling classes. Their old King, George III, now blind and mad, still occupied the throne; his fat son, the vain, talented Prince Regent, was unpopular and so was the government, but the aristocracy continued to rule the country. The rich were richer than ever and the poor still toiled long hours in field and factory.

During the years following Waterloo, Britain learned something of the turmoil that had affected the nations of Europe. Unemployment, dear bread and taxes on food and drink led to discontent and riots. Angry crowds attacked factories to smash the machines which seemed to have taken away their jobs and eleven persons were killed at 'Peterloo' when soldiers tried to disperse a meeting in St Peter's Field, Manchester. Rumours of armed gatherings and talk of revolution alarmed the government. But Britain was not as desperate as Louis XVI's France. Poverty and injustice existed on every side but the workers had not reached such depths of misery that they were ready to kill their masters. In any case, they lacked leaders and were forbidden to form unions or even to hold meetings. The situation grew quieter as trade picked up and jobs became more plentiful.

Coal and iron had turned Britain into an industrial nation. These were the materials that made it possible to produce the goods that the world wanted – clothes, hardware, machinery, pottery, guns and glass. As industry gathered pace, a speedier method was needed to carry goods about the country and down to the ports. Canal-barges were slow and horse-drawn wagons were slower still. Great efforts were made to improve the roads and John Macadam and Thomas Telford were busily engaged on laying their new highways when a young man named Stephenson went to the mining village of Wylam, near Newcastle, to look at a moving steam-engine named *Puffing Billy*.

George Stephenson came from a family so poor that he was out to work at eight years of age, and at fourteen he was earning a man's wage of a shilling a day for looking after a pumping-engine. Unable to read and write until he was grown up, the lad had the born engineer's gift to take engines to pieces and to make them work better. This was why he went to watch *Puffing Billy* pull coal trucks along an iron track.

There had been various attempts to build steam locomotives long before Stephenson ever saw one, but most people regarded them as extravagant oddities. Horses were cheaper and much more reliable. Stephenson, however, became convinced that he could build an efficient locomotive and with help from his employers he constructed one named *Blücher*. It was far from perfect but good enough to encourage the idea of a railway that would carry goods and passengers. Given the post of chief engineer, Stephenson laid the track from Stockton

to Darlington in Durham and, just ten years after Waterloo he himself drove the first train along it at the
astounding speed of 12 mph. When his locomotive, *The
Rocket*, beat all its rivals for service on the new Manchester to Liverpool line, the Railway Age had begun.

People tumbled over each other in their eagerness to
subscribe money to buy land and to hire the gangs of
labourers who laid the tracks along which Stephenson's
engines were to run. Within twenty years Britain had
the world's first railway network, with over 5,000 miles
of track, signalling and electric telegraph systems and a
high standard of service and speed. This remarkable
achievement which changed life in Britain more rapidly
than any other happening in history, owed almost everything to one man. Hardly anywhere, at home or abroad,
was the building of a railway contemplated without
'Geordie' Stephenson's advice. His *Rocket* was the
father of every other steam-locomotive that ever ran, for
its design provided the basic principle of steam loco-
motion during the 120 years when steam ruled the
world's railways.

HELP FOR THE POOR

SUCH rapid changes in transport and industry brought fortunes to a few and a better standard of life to a great many others. The changes also brought suffering. In the enthusiasm for 'progress', there was no time to bother about those who were too weak or too young to defend themselves. Thus, men worked for wages that barely kept them alive, women and girls dragged coal-trucks in the mines and children were sent to the factories almost as soon as they could walk, since even the smallest could earn a few pence for crawling under machines to clean the parts.

In return for their labour, the poor lived worse than animals. It seemed to be nobody's concern that the children grew up bent and diseased, that a great part of the nation was under-nourished, ignorant and dirty. Indeed, most people believed that it would be wrong to interfere with the laws of nature. The poor must stay poor because if wages went up, profits would fall, business would dry up and everyone would be ruined.

Here and there a few people refused to accept this comfortable notion. Robert Owen, himself a poor boy who went to work at seven and supported himself entirely from the age of ten, became part-owner and manager of a huge spinning-mill at New Lanark in Scotland. His pity was roused by the condition of the child-workers, most of them orphans and foundlings sent from the workhouses to toil for thirteen or fourteen hours a day for six and a half days a week in the hot, damp atmosphere of a cotton-mill. Owen shocked public opinion by providing better houses and cheaper food for his workers; he encouraged them to be clean and honest, he paid them higher wages and opened a school for the children. People declared him mad. His soft-headed ideas would bring ruin to his partners, and although Owen proved that better wages and conditions could still produce good profits, he was regarded as a crank for the rest of his life. Certainly most of his later plans failed and he lost his fortune, but his ideas lived on and the workers never forgot him.

There were others, besides Owen, who cared about the poor. John Wesley travelled the country for fifty years, preaching to outdoor congregations of miners, weavers, spinners, foundrymen, fishermen and labourers. He suffered persecution and his life was often in danger. Besides bringing religion and a new sense of self-respect and decency to hundreds of thousands of workers who had never entered a church, he also helped to found schools and orphanages.

A man from an entirely different background from Owen was Anthony Ashley Cooper, the seventh Earl of Shaftesbury. Born into a rich aristocratic family, he grew up with the same passionate determination to put right some of the evils of his time. He believed that the best way to do this was to change some of the laws and to bring in new ones, and after years of ridicule and abuse, he persuaded Parliament to reduce factory hours of work to ten hours a day for most workers and less for young children, to stop women and children working underground in the mines and to forbid the employment of little boys as chimney-sweeps. Outside Parliament, 'our Earl' , as the workers called Shaftesbury, did much to help the men and women who had started the 'Ragged Schools' for the homeless waifs who lived in the streets. Like Elizabeth Fry, who forced people to feel ashamed of the inhuman treatment of lunatics and prisoners, and like countless other Victorians who refused to accept injustice as a normal part of life, Shaftesbury was upheld by a deep religious faith.

During the 1840's, the 'Hungry Forties', there occurred the Irish Famine, when a then unknown disease destroyed the potatoes on which the vast majority of the Irish lived. More than a million died of starvation and almost as many again emigrated to the United States and Canada. This tragedy convinced Sir Robert Peel, the prime minister, that he must abolish the Corn Laws so that foreign corn could come readily into the country.

In this way, he hoped to help the poor by bringing down the price of bread.

Abolishing the Corn Laws ruined Peel's career and did nothing to help the Irish or the poor. The price of wheat remained much the same and Ireland's plight was as desperate as ever. In the rest of Britain, however, conditions began to improve when a trade boom and a number of good harvests made life easier for the workers.

QUEEN VICTORIA

AS the old Duke of Wellington remarked, the country
was 'getting on to its legs again'. Business picked up, the
railways were still expanding and the ports were crammed with British goods on their way to customers over-
seas, for by now Britain was selling more than all the
other nations put together. The empire was growing
bigger and richer, as small wars and annexations
brought fresh territories in India, Africa and the Pacific
under British rule.

Wealth flowed into Britain. It failed to reach the
poorest class but increasing numbers of the people came
to have a share in the country's progress. They were
proud of their success and felt that old 'Pam', Lord Pal-
merston, was quite right when he bullied foreign governments and made them understand Britain's power.

More thoughtful people considered that the British had a special mission to bring justice and good government to those unfortunate countries which had never known these blessings. This sense of belonging to a gifted, superior nation was increased by a changed attitude towards the crown.

When William IV died, he was succeeded by his niece, Princess Victoria. She was only eighteen but although in childhood she had been over-sheltered by a domineering mother, she at once behaved with remarkable dignity and charm. In place of the Hanoverians whom no one could admire, the people now had a vivacious girl on the throne who was painstakingly anxious to be a good and dutiful Queen. It was not long before Victoria married Prince Albert, a German cousin, and although her serious-minded husband was never popular, their marriage was blissfully successful. Family happiness and an earnest interest in the country's affairs took the place of the old scandals and quarrels. The court became respectable and dull, for Albert shared none of the Queen's natural gaiety. Unfortunately, his early death reduced her to such a state of gloom that it seemed as if she had retired into perpetual mourning. However, when she was older, she fell under the spell of the witty and amusing prime minister, Benjamin Disraeli, who coaxed her into reappearing in public; and by the latter part of her immensely long reign, this obstinate, astute little woman had earned for the royal family an affectionate respect so deep that it has never since been seriously weakened.

A WAR AND A MUTINY

DURING Queen Victoria's reign, there were one or two setbacks to the British people's self-confidence. Having become accustomed to the idea that they managed all things better than anyone else, they were shocked to discover that when it came to war, their army was wretchedly equipped and badly led.

The Crimean War was fought to prevent Russia overthrowing the Turkish Empire, and all the fighting took place in the Crimea, a part of southern Russia where the British and their French allies attempted to capture the Black Sea port of Sebastopol. Troops, many of them sent from India, were landed in summer kit, without the supplies, tents, greatcoats and boots that were needed to sustain them through the Russian winter. Bad as the arrangements were for the fighting-men, they were even worse for the sick and wounded. The base hospital was miles away across the Black Sea where, in a filthy ruinous barracks, men died like flies from fever, frostbite, and sheer neglect. In the entire place, there was not a bandage, a bowl, a bottle of medicine or even a spoon. All had been forgotten or had never arrived.

For the first time in history, thanks to the recently

invented electric telegraph, the public were able to read up-to-date reports of the war in their newspapers. They read how the soldiers fought with matchless courage at Alma and Inkerman, and how the Light Brigade charged so gloriously and uselessly at Balaclava. With mounting anger, they also read of the shocking conditions in which these brave fellows were forced to live and die. The public indignation brought results. Stores and equipment were dispatched to the front and money was collected to send out a team of nurses under the leadership of the only woman in England with expert knowledge of hospitals and nursing.

In the eyes of her parents and of most Victorians, Miss Florence Nightingale was an extremely odd person. Brought up to the leisured life of a rich young lady, she had insisted upon having a career, and against her family's wishes she had gone abroad to study nursing, an occupation which was normally followed only by the lowest and most ignorant of women. By the time of the Crimean War, she had become lady-superintendent of a London hospital for sick gentlewomen, and it was therefore to Miss Nightingale that the government turned when it decided to send out a party of nurses to look after the wounded.

Knowing a great deal about how to overcome stupidity and prejudice, she arrived at the hospital base of Scutari in Turkey. The hostility of the army authorities did not dismay her any more than the filth and stench of that vast barracks where the sick and the dead lay side by side on floors oozing with damp. She pursed her mouth and waited for the army to seek her assistance. The arrival of fresh shiploads of wounded turned a difficult situation into chaos and in desperation the army officers turned to the fierce little woman in a black dress with white collar and cuffs. At least she had thirty-eight nurses and large sums of money to buy all the stores that were needed.

Miss Nightingale took command. Her first action was to produce not medicine but two hundred scrubbing-brushes. Floors and walls were scoured, barrow-loads of filth were wheeled away, a kitchen was opened to cook decent food for the men, a laundry was organized to wash their bedding and lice-ridden shirts, and fresh air was let into the entire place. Then she began to nurse the sick. As one of the wounded soldiers said, 'We felt we were in Heaven . . . What a comfort it was to see her pass even. . . . We lay there in hundreds but we could kiss her shadow as it fell.' Those in authority found her a hard and efficient organizer with a sharp tongue and a ruthless knack of geting her own way, but all the tenderness and compassion in her nature went out to those broken men who lay waiting for her to come to them. 'I became,' she said, 'mother to 50,000 soldiers.' She not only nursed them but wrote their letters, saved their pay, sent it home to their wives and made them regard themselves as decent human beings.

Florence Nightingale wrought a miracle, not only because she saved the lives of hundreds of men for whom she almost died from camp fever, but because, by her example and ceaseless work for the next fifty years, she transformed hospitals and the nursing profession. She was also one of the little band of enthusiasts who, like Elizabeth Garrett Anderson, the first woman doctor, made it possible for women to have education and careers.

Hardly had the Crimean War ended than the nation was shocked to learn of a violent uprising in the empire. The Indian Mutiny affected only a small part of the huge continent where British rule was accepted by millions of the inhabitants. To the vast majority, the

British brought peaceful, orderly government and their rule was opposed chiefly by the warlike tribesmen who lived by pillaging their neighbours, and by religious leaders who did not wish the people's ancient customs and beliefs to be interfered with. The mutiny was sparked off by what seemed to be an insult to religion.

The army, which contained a great many Indian soldiers, known as sepoys, was issued with a new rifle cartridge coated with grease. Rumour had it that the grease was made from the fat of cows, animals sacred to the Hindus, or from the fat of pigs, animals considered unclean by the followers of Mohammed, or from a mixture of both. Aided by an old prophecy that the British were due to be ousted from India that very year, the rumour provoked a regiment to mutiny. At Meerut the sepoys killed their officers and were joined by more soldiers, freed prisoners and some of the populace. They laid siege to Delhi, Cawnpore and Lucknow. At Cawnpore a massacre took place, but Delhi and Lucknow held out until fresh troops arrived to relieve the hard-

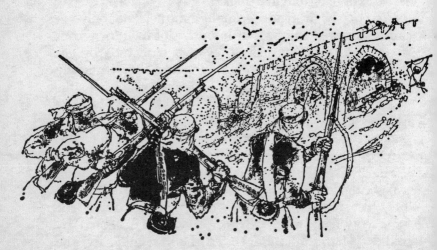

pressed defenders and presently to subdue the entire province. As a result of the mutiny, the powers of the old East India Company were taken over by the British government and the Queen appointed a Viceroy to rule in her absence. The huge country settled down again to ninety years of fairly peaceful government.

The handful of British officials and soldiers who ruled India and the rest of the empire made mistakes and were sometimes guilty of arrogance and tactlessness, but most of them were filled with an honourable desire to do their duty. They believed that it was their mission to bring civilized justice to backward peoples and it was with ideals of service and adventure that so many hundreds of young men set off to distant parts of the world.

LIVINGSTONE IN AFRICA

AUSTRALIA, New Zealand, the Pacific Islands, Burma and the coastal fringe of China attracted adventurers and settlers in search of land, gold and trade. Some wanted none of these things. They were the explorers and missionaries, and Africa, more than anywhere else, drew them like a magnet.

North Africa and the coastal regions of East and West Africa had been known for centuries, and in the south the Dutch had founded a colony which was by now under British rule, but the heart of Africa was a vast continent unknown to Europeans.

The first probings into the interior were made during the Napoleonic wars by a group of wealthy Englishmen interested in geography. They sent out Mungo Park to explore the River Niger and presently the government provided money to further exploration which fired the enthusiasm of Victorian gentlemen for 'Christianity and commerce'. Missionary societies were founded and early in Queen Victoria's reign there arrived at Cape Town a young man named David Livingstone.

Born in poverty near Glasgow, Livingstone had taught himself Latin at ten years of age as he stood at work in a cotton mill. By intense efforts, he passed his examinations to become a doctor of medicine and his intention was to serve as a missionary in China. By chance, however, he turned one evening into a meeting-hall where a returned missionary was speaking of his work in South Africa. When Livingstone heard him say, 'On a clear morning, I can see from the hills of Kuruman, the smoke of a thousand villages where no missionary has ever been,' he made up his mind that he would carry the Gospel and his medical knowledge to the Africans.

After working for a time at a mission station 100 miles upcountry, Livingstone travelled farther north to start a new missionary settlement in country which had never before seen a white man. Here, with the aid of his wife Mary, he won the friendship of the native people who willingly acted as guides on his journeys to distant kraals where he preached and tended the sick. The urge to go farther and farther on took him across the dreaded Kalahari Desert and then, having made a nightmare journey with his wife and babies in an ox-wagon, he left them in the care of a friendly chief and pushed on alone to the great Zambesi River. Reluctantly, he decided that the climate was too unhealthy for his family and that he must see them safely off to England before he could explore further. After accompanying them to Cape Town, he made the immense journey back to Linyanti, in the heart of Africa.

With a few stores crammed into a tin box and some of his black friends as escorts, Livingstone set out westwards towards 'the white man's sea'. For months they travelled along rivers, through forests and across great grasslands and by the time they reached the ocean, fever

and hunger had reduced Livingstone almost to a skele-
ton. After a period for rest, he set out again to keep his
promise to return his faithful tribesmen to their chief.
The journey took a year but having reached Linyanti,
he continued eastwards down the Zambesi towards the
Indian Ocean, discovering the Victoria Falls on the way
and passing through a country terrorized by the Arab
slave-dealers. In four years he had explored and mapped
a huge area of Africa, and on his return to England his
book about his travels not only made him a public hero

but led to a wave of enthusiasm for African exploration.
The Royal Geographical Society sent out Burton and
Speke to find the source of the Nile and paid the expenses
of Livingstone's next expedition which was to last for
five years.

After this, he could have retired to enjoy the fortune
which his books had earned but Africa drew him back.
His wife had died of fever and the gaunt missionary
spent another six years exploring the upper reaches of
the Congo in Central Africa. His last journey was made

in order to map the huge tract of land between Zanzibar
and Lake Tanganyika. When he set out with Susi, his
black servant, and several others, the doctor was far
from well, for the strain of his journeys and innumerable
bouts of fever had weakened even his tough frame. The
going was exceptionally difficult and the loss of his medicine chest meant that he could no longer control the
fever. Too weak to walk during the last part of the
journey, he was carried on a litter made from boughs
until they reached Ujiji on the shore of Lake Tanganyika. Here, at the centre of the Arab slave-trade, he
recovered sufficiently to begin exploring the surrounding
country and to encourage the inhabitants to resist the
slavers.

For four years no news of Livingstone reached the
outside world and public alarm reached such a pitch that
an American newspaper sent out an expedition led by an
adventurous reporter named H. M. Stanley. Following
every clue that he could pick up in East Africa, Stanley
eventually tracked the missing hero to Ujiji. News of the
approaching party of strangers had been carried ahead
and Stanley had to push his way through a crowd of
excited Africans to enter the village. He saw a tall,
bearded white man standing outside a hut. He looked ill
and confused by the commotion. Stanley advanced
towards him, took off his hat and said: 'Dr Livingstone,
I presume?'

The two men liked each other and Stanley, who had
himself known great hardship in his early life and was
presently to become a celebrated explorer, did everything possible to nurse the sick doctor back to health and
to persuade him to go home. It was no use. 'I must finish
my task,' said Livingstone.

With the new stores, he set out on another journey of
exploration but his strength had gone, and one morning

Susi found that his master had died in the night kneeling in prayer by his bed. In loving sorrow, his black servants buried his heart beside Lake Bangweolo and then they wrapped his body in bark and carried it a thousand miles to the coast so that his own countrymen could bury him in Westminster Abbey.

Not all the white men who ventured into Africa's interior came with the ideals of Livingstone. Besides the traders and the diamond- and gold-prospectors, there were the riff-raff of a dozen nations, all on the look-out for a living by any means whatsoever. In the south, the Dutch settlers, known as Boers, were dour, Old Testament-reading farmers, who believed that the black people were an inferior race ordained by providence to work for the white man. Resentful at British rule and at the arrival of missionaries, many of the Boers decided to leave Cape Colony and to trek north into the vast grasslands of the interior where they could raise cattle and live without interference.

Thus the Boer republics of the Transvaal and the Orange Free State came into existence, but it was not long before the Boers, in their widely scattered farms, found themselves unable to control the warlike Zulus. Reluctantly, they had to accept Britain's annexation of the Transvaal. The Zulus proved to be formidable warriors and it was only after some setbacks and hard fighting that the British troops managed to defeat their chief, Cetewayo. At once, the Boers clamoured for the return of their independence and this was granted by Mr Gladstone, leader of the Liberals.

GLADSTONE AND DISRAELI

WILLIAM EWART GLADSTONE had recently
become prime minister after waging a thunderous elec-
tion campaign against his rival, Disraeli. At a time when
there were no sporting heroes or popular stars, people
took a tremendous interest in parliamentary affairs and
they followed the contest between these two politicians
with as much excitement as if it had been a heavyweight
boxing championship.

Speeches in the House of Commons were reported in
full in the daily newspapers, were discussed, read aloud
and argued over in homes and public-houses. Year in
and year out, the battle between Gladstone and Disraeli
seemed, to their separate supporters, to be no less than a
fight between good and evil.

Disraeli, leader of the Conservatives, was a Jew who
had started his career without money or aristocratic

connections. Yet he had arrived at the head of the party
which represented wealth and the traditional right of
the English gentry to rule the country. When he first
entered Parliament, his appearance and manner
aroused such ridicule that he was forced to bring his first
speech to an end with these words: 'I will sit down now
but the time will come when you will hear me!' Everything about him seemed to offend the Conservatives –
his foreign name and appearance, his dandified clothes
(he often wore green trousers, fancy waistcoats and an
assortment of rings and watchchains), his black hair ar-
ranged into a curl on his forehead and, above all, his cool
and venomously witty manner of speaking. But the
brilliant outsider triumphed. After Peel fell from office,
Disraeli rebuilt the Conservative party and gave it a new
policy – growth of British power abroad and improve-
ment in the people's lives at home. When, as he said, he
'climbed to the top of the greasy pole' to become prime
minister, he won Queen Victoria's confidence to an
extraordinary degree. Flattering her, making her laugh
with his amusing anecdotes, he drew her back into
public life, so that she came to dote upon the dazzling
charmer who brought her the title of Empress of India
and secured the Suez Canal for Britain.

Her affection for 'Dizzy' was matched by her dislike
for Gladstone. The great Liberal, to whom politics were
part of his religion, was never at ease in the Queen's
presence. As solemn and awe-inspiring as one of the ancient prophets, he spoke as if he were addressing a vast
audience, fixing them with his piercing gaze as the
tremendous sentences rolled over them like a flood.
Queen Victoria did not like being lectured and she made
no attempt to conceal her exasperation with Gladstone's
manner and opinions.

'The Grand Old Man', as his supporters called him,

bore the sovereign's dislike with patience, for nothing could change his views of what was right. He believed in reform and progress, with peace abroad and justice for the weaker nations. Thus, he wanted the Irish to be allowed to rule themselves and he was opposed to the use of force and the expansion of the empire.

WAR IN SOUTH AFRICA

IN keeping with his principles, Gladstone had restored independence to the Boers when an event took place which changed the situation in South Africa. Gold was discovered in Transvaal and a horde of adventurers poured into the farming province in search of fortunes. The gold-rush town of Johannesburg sprang up over-night and the newcomers, mostly British, soon out-numbered the Boers. In fear of losing control of the country, the Boer president, Paul Kruger, refused to give the newcomers – the 'Uitlanders' – the right to vote, though they were made to pay heavy taxes.

By this time the most commanding figure in South Africa was Cecil Rhodes. He had come out from England after leaving school and by luck and ability had made a fortune in the diamond-fields before he was twenty. Immensely rich and eager for power, 'Rhodes was also an idealist who loved Africa and genuinely believed that its black peoples would be happiest under British rule. With all the zest of his masterful character, he set to work to make his dream come true of an English-speaking land that would stretch from Cape Town to Cairo. The Boers, whom he despised, presented a stumbling-block to his plans. Having used his influence as prime minister of Cape Colony to extend British territory to the south and west of the Boer republics, Rhodes formed a company to develop a huge expanse of almost uninhabited territory lying north of Transvaal. A railway line was built to provide a link with Cape Town and settlers began to move into the new country which was presently named Rhodesia.

The Boers naturally regarded these activities with alarm. Knowing that Rhodes owned a large share of the gold mines in Transvaal, they rightly suspected that his next move would be an attempt to gain control of their country. With his friend, Dr Jameson, Rhodes concocted a plan to bring about an uprising of the Uitlanders in Johannesburg. At the head of a small force of mounted police, Jameson was to make an armed dash into Transvaal but the plans went wrong and Jameson's Raid was a sensational failure. A few of the mounted raiders were killed and the rest surrendered, so that the only results were to put an end to Rhodes' career and to inflame the bad feeling between the Boers and the British. Emboldened by this success and by offers of German weapons, the Boers made preparations to drive the British clean out of South Africa. They could

put 60,000 resolute, well-mounted marksmen into the
field against fewer than 15,000 British regulars and
when Kruger learned that reinforcements had been
ordered to the Cape, he sent a truculent demand for
their recall and followed this up by ordering an attack
on British territory.

The war began with a series of disasters for Britain
which reached their peak in 'Black Week' when an astonished world learned that the forces of the most
powerful empire in history had been defeated three times
by the Boer farmers of two tiny republics. What was more
surprising, however, was the Boer failure to follow up
their early successes. They had superior numbers, far
better artillery, and hosts of supporters and Dutch relatives in the British territories. Instead of sweeping
through to the Cape, they wasted time and effort on
besieging the little towns of Kimberley, Mafeking and
Ladysmith.

This mistake gave the British time to bring in reinforcements. The garrisons of the three towns held out
until the new commanders, Lord Roberts and Lord
Kitchener, were able to counter-attack. Kimberley and
Ladysmith were relieved and as the Boers retreated, a
British column advanced towards Mafeking, the most
northerly outpost. This small town had been completely
surrounded for months but its small garrison was commanded by Colonel Baden-Powell with such courage
and bluff that it was able to withstand enemy attacks and
all the privations of a siege for 217 days.

The relief of Mafeking caused a tremendous outburst
of joy in London but it did not end the war. With Pre-
toria, their capital, taken and Kruger a fugitive, the
Boers still refused to surrender. Guerilla 'commandos'
under Botha, De Wet and Smuts defied Kitchener for
nearly two years, roaming the vast country, attacking

British posts and drawing supplies and information from the scattered farms. It was impossible to surround or catch them and in the end Kitchener found there was no answer except to destroy their farms and put their families into camps.

At last peace was made on terms which brave men could accept. Though nothing could bring back the children who had died in the camps, a gift of three million pounds was made by Britain to restore the farms and the two Boer republics were promised self-government at an early date.

EDWARDIAN DAYS

THE war was still dragging towards its end when Queen Victoria died. During her reign of more than sixty-three years, Britain had advanced to the summit of power and influence in the world and people rightly supposed that the old Queen's death had brought an age to its close.

Some of them feared that the reputation of the crown would decline, for the new monarch, 'a jolly old sport' to his more vulgar subjects, was chiefly known for his love of racehorses and pretty women. However, Edward VII at once showed that his mother had been wrong to distrust his ability for so many years. Besides taking up his duties with regal dignity, he helped to bring about a friendly understanding with France and took an astute interest in the country's affairs. The outlook seemed better than ever. There was a lively, more cheerful spirit in the country, an air of prosperous content and a new government full of plans to improve the lives of working people.

All kinds of inventions and devices appeared to point to an increase in progress and happiness. Motor-cars, developed at first in Germany and France, were now being made in England, for the law which required a man to walk ahead of a motor-car carrying a red flag had been repealed and the King himself was an enthusiastic motorist. Two brothers named Wright built a flying-machine in America that actually flew and this exciting news was soon followed by the appearance in the sky of aeroplanes and gliders. For less adventurous people, there were bicycles with rubber tyres, cheap railway trips to the seaside, electric tramcars and underground trains, moving pictures in the first cinemas and the voices of celebrated singers issuing from gramophone horns. There was scientific progress, too, with marvellous discoveries such as wireless, radium and X-rays which added to the sense of adventure aroused by the almost superhuman qualities of endurance displayed by the Antarctic heroes, Shackleton and Scott. At a less exciting level, new schools and public libraries were being built and workers began to have a weekly half-holiday.

Further improvements in the people's everyday lives were introduced by the new Liberal government which was probably the most talented and civilized government this country has ever had. Led by Mr Asquith, a clever, aloof lawyer, the Liberals brought in old-age pensions, unemployment pay, sick benefits, labour exchanges and a host of lesser reforms to help those who were poor and unfortunate. To carry out the main part of this programme, Asquith appointed two ministers who were to prove themselves the outstanding politicians of the century. They came from utterly different backgrounds but they resembled each other in the force of their personalities, in their ambition and driving determination to get things done. Their names were David Lloyd George and Winston Churchill.

David Lloyd George was brought up in a Welsh village in the house of his uncle, a cobbler who was a local preacher and a man of strong character. The boy went

to the village school and showed such brilliance that his uncle decided that he should become a lawyer. Since there was no one to teach him Latin and French, uncle and nephew slogged painfully through grammar-books and dictionaries until David had learned sufficient to be able to pass his first Law examination and to enter a firm of solicitors. He lived in lodgings, working in an office by day and studying by candlelight at night until, after six years, he was ready to take his final examination in London. Whilst there, he visited the House of Commons and saw his idol, Mr Gladstone, rise to make a speech. One day, he vowed, he too would speak in Parliament.

There followed several years of building up a solicitor's practice, mostly for people as poor as he had been, and when he was elected to Parliament by 18 votes, he had to give up most of his income, for in those days M.P.s were not paid. The short, good-looking Welshman with a great mane of hair quickly made an impression upon the House. On Welsh affairs, temperance and religious matters, he spoke with passionate eloquence, but he was still a back-bencher, without influence or powerful friends, and the Liberals had small hopes of taking office. Then came the Boer War and young Lloyd George appeared to have ruined his career. In the face of the nation's aggressive patriotism, he sided with the Boers and became so unpopular that on one occasion he narrowly escaped death at the hands of an enraged crowd.

The war and the public's anger passed away and when a Liberal government was elected, Lloyd George had risen to become one of its leading members. His chance had come and he seized it eagerly. At the Board of Trade and presently as Chancellor of the Exchequer, he worked like a dynamo to bring in reforms which would help the poor, the old and the unemployed. In this work, which infuriated his political enemies, he was supported by his admiring colleague, Winston Churchill.

Churchill had known nothing of the older man's poverty and struggle. Born into an aristocratic family, son of the brilliant Lord Randolph Churchill and educated at a famous school, Winston was a dunce. He would not or could not learn sufficient Latin to make any advance and his sole achievements were in reciting poetry and in fencing. In despair, his father sent him into the army where, to everyone's surprise, he did rather well and was posted as a cavalry officer to India. Here, he distinguished himself in several ways. He not only became a crack polo player but he actually began to educate himself, reading with an appetite he had never showed at school and beginning to write articles for newspapers at home. This occupation put him into hot water with his superiors for, after taking part in a campaign against the tribesmen of the North West Frontier, he had the nerve to write a book criticizing the commanders. A

desire to be present wherever things were happening took
him next to Egypt where he got himself attached to
Kitchener's army in the campaign to conquer the Sudan
and he charged with the cavalry at Omdurman.

Having quitted the army, Churchill went to South
Africa as a war-correspondent and was captured by the
Boers after displaying much courage during an attack
on an armoured train. His thrilling escape from a pris-
oner-of-war camp made world-wide news and, as a
public hero, he came home to stand for Parliament. It
was not long before this high-spirited fellow was in the
Liberal government, working heart and soul alongside
Lloyd George and subduing for the time being his military interests in favour of workmen's hours and in-
surance.

In their efforts to deal with poverty and injustice at
home, the Liberals tended to overlook affairs outside
Britain and it was suddenly and, it seemed, by accident
that they found themselves at war.

THE GREAT WAR

IN a dusty little town named Sarajevo, a Serbian student shot and killed the Archduke Ferdinand of Austria. Violence was common enough in Balkan politics and the crime aroused interest but no alarm in London. Austria, however, saw in the assassination the opportunity to destroy Serbia, a Balkan country which had long been an irritating obstacle to her aims in that part of Europe. The Austrian threats to Serbia were supported by Germany. But Russia regarded herself as the Serbs' champion and would go to the rescue if an attack were made. This would bring in France, because she was Russia's ally and had not Britain made a friendly agreement with France?

In this complicated situation, there were a few who realized that the murder at Sarajevo could lead to a world war. But in Britain most people dismissed the danger. Why should they go to war because of a quarrel in the Balkans? Talks were starting and the trouble would soon blow over.

But the real cause of the trouble lay much deeper. For forty years, Germany had been growing stronger and

more truculent. Her people were told that, whereas
other nations had empires and world-wide trade they,
the cleverest and most hardworking people in Europe,
had been left out in the cold. The chief culprits were
Britain and France who greedily refused to share the
good things of the earth and so, while the German
Kaiser, Queen Victoria's grandson, swaggered and
boasted, his generals prepared for war. Their plan was
simple. The German armies would sweep through Belgium and France with a great scything blow that would
crush France so swiftly that the campaign would be over
before her ally Russia could move. The British, strong
only at sea, would be powerless to interfere. By 1914 the
German generals were ready and the murder at Sarajevo provided the excuse that was needed.

At the mention of Belgium, however, the mood of the
British people changed. Britain, like Germany and all
the great powers, had agreed that Belgium should be
neutral and no armies should ever invade her territory.
Yet the Germans were proposing to ignore the rights of a
small country which had not given the slightest offence.
For the British, this was enough. They cared nothing for
the Serbs or the Russians; the agreement with France
had been hidden from them but the attack on 'brave little
Belgium' affronted their sense of fair play. Almost to a
man, they agreed that they must fight to teach the bully
a lesson. The navy, thanks to Churchill, was at action
stations and with the confidence of a nation which had
always triumphed, they believed it would 'all be over by
Christmas'.

The most deadly war in the world's history lasted for
more than four years and cost the lives of ten million
soldiers and of countless civilians. Yet it was indeed
almost over in the first few weeks. The German armies
swept into France and came close to Paris before the

French and, on their left, the small but superb British
army held firm, checked the onslaught and drove the
enemy back to the River Aisne.

Then there developed a war which not even the generals had foreseen. The destructive force of heavy artillery and the murderous power of machine-gun fire made
it impossible for the armies to stand up and fight, so they
dug themselves into the earth in trenches that stretched
across France from the Alps to the sea. To get at their
enemy, soldiers had to clamber into the open, and cross
'no-man's land' towards a forest of barbed wire protect-
ing the opposite trenches. The defenders invariably
mowed down the attackers and those who did manage

to reach the enemy line found that there were other lines
behind with strongpoints and communication-trenches
making an impassable network of defence. The old ways
of fighting with cavalry and outflanking movements were
useless and so the soldiers dug themselves in and endured
the mud and the shelling, the big attacks which the
generals felt obliged to launch, the appalling loss of life
and the tragic farce of trying to break an unbreakable
deadlock.

All kinds of efforts were made for victory. The
Germans used poison gas, the Allies developed the first
tanks and failed to employ them properly; both sides
relied on gigantic artillery bombardments and on
trying to starve the other's civilian population. Aeroplanes which began as scouts turned to bombing, submarines became deadlier than surface warships, fresh
allies were dragged in until half the world was engaged
in the struggle and entire nations gave up everything in
order to produce guns, shells and yet more armies for the
slaughter.

In eastern Europe, the war was less like a siege but
equally bloody. The huge, ill-armed, badly commanded
Russian armies blundered to and fro, suffering terrible
defeats from the Germans but almost crushing the Austrians and their allies. The need to help Russia, whose
soldiers went into action sometimes without even a rifle
apiece, led to an attempt to break into south-east
Europe. Lloyd George and Churchill both favoured the
idea of an attack through the Balkans but it was
Churchill's plan to capture Constantinople that won
grudging approval. The naval attack on the Dardanelles
failed narrowly and by the time troops were landed on
Gallipoli shore, the plan was doomed. Surprise had
gone, the Turks fought stubbornly and the generals in
France had never released sufficient men to give the

landings a chance. The bold stroke became a heart-breaking failure and Churchill left the government to return to soldiering in France.

As Churchill fell and Asquith's authority faded, Lloyd George came to power. The war was going badly, for Gallipoli was followed by gigantic losses on the Western front, where the French were badly weakened and the British were short of shells and ammunition. At sea, the German fleet was brought to battle at Jutland, only to escape into the darkness after inflicting some unexpected damage to the British ships and, shortly afterwards, Lord Kitchener, the veteran hero, was drowned at sea.

The one man who seemed as full of confidence as ever was Lloyd George. By forceful methods, he made the factories produce an ever-increasing flow of war-supplies and it seemed to many people that here was the leader the country needed. Asquith was ousted and Lloyd George took his place as Prime Minister. To many Liberals this was treachery and they never forgave him. King George V disliked the 'Welsh Wizard', Haig, the commander-in-chief, and most of the generals detested him and there were good reasons for many others to distrust him. He was tricky and vain, dangerous to his enemies and faithless to his friends but he was also a great man, with a genius for getting impossible things done, for overcoming difficulties and for driving on in the face of every setback. He was called 'the man who won the war' and he deserved the name.

Mass warfare threw up very few heroes at the top. In the long bitter struggle, there were hardly any successes but countless losses and disappointments; Haig was too silent to be popular, Churchill and Admiral Beatty both possessed courage and flair but no luck, and one of the very few who caught the public's imagination was an eccentric archaeologist named T. E. Lawrence who aided the Arab revolt against the Turks, though the real victor was General Allenby. In truth, the heroes of the war were the soldiers in the trenches and the seamen who braved the submarines to keep Britain from starvation.

After three years, the collapse of Russia, near-mutiny in the French army, the defeat of the Italians and disastrous losses of merchant-ships brought the allies almost to their knees. The Germans, strengthened by their armies from the Eastern Front, then launched a series of tremendous attacks mainly upon the British, drove them back and actually broke right through into open country. Once again, they came within striking distance of Paris, but, once again, the allies, now under a supreme commander, Marshal Foch, held out as fresh American troops began to arrive in ever-increasing numbers. When exhaustion brought the German advance to a halt, Foch and Haig took their chance to hit back at the most vulnerable parts of the enemy front. The Germans retired fighting but the allies, scenting victory, kept up the pressure so remorselessly that they swept on until suddenly it was clear that the enemy was in full retreat towards his own frontier. Like magic, Austria, Turkey and Bulgaria collapsed, the German fleet mutinied, civilians rioted in Germany, the Kaiser fled to Holland and the war was over.

BETWEEN THE WARS

VICTORY had come at last but, as in the years after Waterloo, it was followed by hard times and suffering. Trade failed to pick up and soon there were a million or more men without jobs.

A tragic struggle now took place in Ireland. Before the war Asquith had been ready to give the Irish the right to rule themselves, and this induced the Protestants of Ulster to declare that they would fight rather than be ruled by a Roman Catholic majority. The war postponed the struggle, but Irish feelings were inflamed by the execution of the leaders of a rising in Dublin. Soon there was no room for moderation, as Irish republicans attacked the police and the British government recruited a force known as the Black and Tans who met terror with terror. At last Lloyd George seemed to have made a settlement when a treaty was signed giving Home Rule to Southern Ireland, but 'the troubles' were not yet over, for civil war broke out between those who accepted the treaty and those who denounced it.

By this time, Lloyd George's great reputation was on

the wane. His popularity was slipping away and there was no loyal party at his back. The Conservatives were tired of a man they had never liked, the Liberals would not rally to him and although Lloyd George remained the ablest politician in the country, he never held office again.

The story of the next seventeen years is a melancholy one of a nation bewildered by its troubles and lack of leadership. Unemployment became a kind of malign bogey which no one seemed to banish, and the very industries on which Britain's prosperity had been founded – coal, iron, cotton and shipbuilding – were the hardest hit. Some parts of the country, South Wales, Lancashire, the North-east and Scotland, became known as Distressed Areas where as many as twenty or thirty men out of every 100 had no work to do. There were strikes, including a General Strike that fizzled out after nine days, hunger-marches and pay-cuts; but unemployment never dropped below a million until the next war made every man's labour necessary.

The country's leaders during this period were Stanley Baldwin, Ramsay MacDonald and Neville Chamberlain, men of more ability and honesty than their critics have allowed but none was great enough to solve the problems at home or to deal with the dangers abroad. Hardly anyone listened to Lloyd George who had positive plans to tackle unemployment, or to Churchill who growled out warnings about Germany's rising strength. Distrusted and frequently derided, they stood on the sidelines watching the lesser men take charge.

The picture was not entirely gloomy during the twenties and thirties, for parts of the country, mainly the Midlands and the south, regained their prosperity thanks to light industries, motor-cars and a great increase in building. Britain still led the world in aircraft

manufacture, civil aviation, car-racing and most kinds of
sport, so that popular heroes included Major Seagrave,
the racing-driver, Jack Hobbs, Lord Nuffield and Amy
Johnson, the girl-pilot from Hull who thrilled everyone
by flying alone to Australia. In science and medicine, Sir
Ernest Rutherford was the pioneer of nuclear physics,
Robert Watson Watt discovered radar, Frank Whittle
invented the jet-engine and Alexander Fleming, a Scot
working at a London hospital, discovered penicillin, the
drug which saved innumerable lives during the Second
World War.

VICTORY AT ALL COSTS

FOR more than a dozen years, people lived in hope that a major war would never happen again. They put their faith in the League of Nations which had been set up at Geneva to settle the nations' quarrels by peaceful discussion and it was not until the thirties when Japan attacked China and the Italian dictator, Mussolini, invaded Abyssinia that they began to realize that the League was powerless to stop the big aggressor. This unhappy truth had already been recognized by Adolf Hitler.

There was nothing in Hitler's early life to suggest that he possessed even average ability, let alone the power to dominate a nation and to commit the most monstrous crimes in the world's history. His schooldays and youth were a story of failure to pass examinations or to secure a regular job and during his service in the 1914–18 War, he rose no higher than the rank of corporal. After the war, this morose day-dreamer joined an obscure political party in Munich where it was discovered at meetings that he did possess one gift. He was an orator who could pour out a torrent of words which had an almost mesmeric effect upon his audience. The message of his

speeches was hatred – hatred of Germany's defeat, of the peace settlement, of socialists, communists and, above all, Jews.

Hitler would probably have continued to be no more than an unpleasant nuisance in Munich had it not been for the Great Depression in world trade. Germany's recovery crashed into ruins; more than six million men became unemployed and, in this situation, people were prepared to listen to a fanatic who claimed to be able to restore the country's greatness. His political party, known as the Nazis, took control of Parliament, and with the aid of a gang of henchmen as wicked and ruthless as their leader, the laws were overthrown, all other parties abolished and all opposition crushed. Hitler became president and commander-in-chief of the German army. He was now a complete dictator, and with terrifying swiftness he put his programme into gear.

Unemployment was overcome by the manufacture of arms, the German army and air force increased at a tremendous rate and, piece by piece, all the losses of the war were recovered. Part of the Rhineland opposite to France was re-occupied by troops, Austria, whose union with Germany was forbidden by the Treaty of Versailles, was taken over, enthusiastic support was given to Mussolini and Franco, the dictators of Italy and Spain, and demands were made on Czechoslovakia to hand over a large part of Czech territory inhabited by German-speaking citizens.

The League of Nations and France and Britain, in particular, watched Hitler's behaviour with nervous dismay. They protested but did little more, partly because their peoples wanted to have nothing to do with war and partly because Hitler outwitted them by constantly promising that each move was his last step towards uniting his country. Many people felt that if Germany's grievances were removed, she would behave sensibly and would see, as they did, that peace was better than war.

This attitude was called 'appeasement' and Neville Chamberlain, the British prime minister, believed in it wholeheartedly. He was sure that if he could meet the dictators face to face, he would talk them into a reasonable frame of mind. So, when Germany's threats to Czechoslovakia seemed about to cause a European war, Chamberlain flew to Munich to meet Hitler. The French prime minister was there, too, and between them they agreed that Czechoslovakia should give Hitler what he wanted. There would be no war and the people of Britain went mad with joyous relief.

But not quite everybody. Churchill pointed out that the unfortunate Czechs had been betrayed and were now defenceless: it was, he said, not a victory but complete and utter defeat.

His words were true. Within six months, Hitler had seized the rest of Czechoslovakia and had begun to threaten Poland. This alarmed even Chamberlain and in a belated effort to stop the aggressor, he promised to support Poland. At this stage the offer was ludicrous and Hitler, who had already made a secret agreement with Russia, knew that no help from Britain and France could reach the Poles. On September 1st, 1939, he invaded Poland and it is said that he was astonished when Britain and France declared themselves at war with Germany.

As in 1914, it was only at the last moment that the British realized that they must fight to prevent one country from dominating Europe. With frantic speed they tried to arm themselves, but neither they nor the French could do anything to prevent the destruction of Poland and, for the first winter, so little happened that this was called the 'phoney war'.

By spring 1940, however, Hitler was ready for his next leap. Norway was invaded and conquered in a few days and, at this, the British people lost all patience with Chamberlain and in reality it was they, and not the politicians, who called in Churchill to take his place. They remembered that he had warned them over and over again of the dangers of appeasement and they knew that although they had derided him as an old war-monger, had questioned his judgement and seen him out of office for many years, he possessed above all else the quality they now needed so badly in a leader – courage. Meanwhile, the Germans had crushed Holland with horrifying speed and their matchless armoured div-isions, their powerful air arm and a huge confident army stood poised to spring at France. The real war had come and Churchill spoke to the nation:

'I have nothing to offer but blood, toil, tears and sweat,' he said. 'You ask, "What is our policy?" I will say: it is to wage war, by sea, land and air, with all our might and with all the strength that God can give us . . . You ask, "What is our aim?" I can answer in one word: Victory – victory at all costs, victory in spite of all terror; victory, however long and hard the road may be.'

There followed the complete collapse of France, the loss of the army's equipment at Dunkirk, the RAF's narrow but decisive victory in the Battle of Britain, the

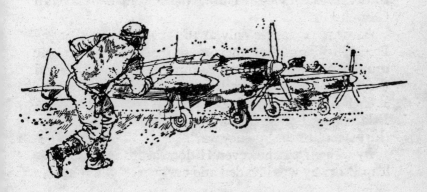

night-bombing, defeat in Greece, Crete and North Africa. By now Britain was alone, still clinging to the hope that Churchill had given them that somehow victory would come. Europe belonged to Hitler and there were more catastrophes to come in the Far East where Singapore, Hong Kong and Burma fell to the Japanese.

Then the tide turned and there were allies fighting the same enemy, not because they came to Britain's rescue but because Hitler attacked Russia and the Japanese destroyed an American fleet at Pearl Harbor. Instead of defeats, there was news of victories – Alamein, Stalingrad and Midway Island. Italy was invaded and at long last the allied armies were back in France, forcing a way in at Normandy and steadily, painfully boring on towards Germany as the Russians closed in from the east. In the end Germany was pounded to defeat and Hitler died in the ruins of Berlin. In 1945 the dropping of two atomic bombs brought the surrender of Japan.

Churchill fulfilled his promise and went out of office immediately he had done so. No single man can win a war. There were other great leaders and generals in the struggle – Roosevelt, Eisenhower, Zhukov, MacArthur and Montgomery – but Churchill saw it through from start to finish and by his will for victory made it possible for other leaders to arise, for the conquered peoples to go on hoping and for the British people to survive. As it happened, it *was* victory at all costs, and costs which are still being paid – economic difficulty, supremacy of the United States, Russian domination of eastern Europe. But Churchill expressed the will of the British people that they should not give in and he showed them, that given courage and leadership, they could achieve miracles, not merely in battle but in the fairer realms of unity, decency and justice. They still can.

INDEX

If you would like to receive a newsletter telling you about our new children's books, fill in the coupon with your name and address and send it to:

Gillian Osband,
Transworld Publishers Ltd,
Century House,
61–63 Uxbridge Road, Ealing,
London, W5 5SA

Name...

Address..

....

CHILDREN'S NEWSLETTER

All the books on the previous pages are available at your bookshop or can be ordered direct from Transworld Publishers Ltd., Cash Sales Dept. P.O. Box 11, Falmouth, Cornwall.

Please send full name and address together with cheque or postal order—no currency, and allow 45p per book to cover postage and packing (plus 20p each for additional copies).